The Ko

*Taking another look at Community,
Discipleship & Service to others*

By Gerrit Gustafson

Contents

© 2019 G235 Communications. Reprint freely except for commercial purposes.

Need more booklets? They are available through amazon.com.

The Koinonia Ethos

Introduction

Imagine

Imagine that every Christian has a circle of at least six or eight faithful friends who walk closely together, who champion God's highest purposes for each other, who sacrifice self interests to see the others succeed, and who help to watch over one another to guard against the schemes of the enemy.

Imagine that, in those circles of friends, God's transforming love and acceptance create an atmosphere of trust where we are no longer afraid to be honest about our deepest needs and our deepest aspirations, where we go beyond the normal superficialities and learn to listen and to speak more deeply with one another.

Imagine that every new believer begins his walk with God in the context of protective care, mentoring and the love of a spiritual family.

Imagine that every Christian receives, in faith, the gifts God is so eager to give, gifts that equip us to grow his kingdom in our midst.

Imagine that every *believer* in Jesus is becoming a true *disciple* of Jesus, ever growing, maturing and generously giving away to others what he has received - that disciples are making disciples - and that the body of Christ is building itself up "as each part does its work."

Imagine that your own life is not just spent pursuing personal success, but in making a difference in the lives of others.

Imagine your particular group of friends gathering with other similar groups so that you not only experience small group intimacy, but the encouragement and vision of larger celebrations.

Imagine the contagion these mini-communities in Christ are creating in their varied spheres of influence as those who look on are attracted by what they see. *Imagine* that evangelism is not just the result of a message spoken, but of a message demonstrated.

You have just imagined true Biblical community, or as Bonhoeffer called it, *life together*.

The Greek word for this kind of togetherness is *koinonia*. It is usually translated in Scripture as *fellowship*, but it has a much deeper meaning than what *fellowship* normally means to us today.

Today's version of *fellowship* is most often casual, incidental and optional. *Koinonia*, in contrast, is committed, intentional and essential. What we call *fellowship* is usually inexpensive, requiring little; *koinonia* is very costly, requiring much. The current understanding of *fellowship* allows us to preserve independence and personal autonomy; *koinonia* doesn't.

When we begin to experience this deep-level belonging, which we're calling *koinonia*, we will most likely have two other amazing experiences: 1) an acceleration of spiritual growth (*Discipleship*), and 2) a release of gifts and ministries through our lives (*Service*).

Koinonia, Discipleship and *Service* - belonging, growing and serving - these three are inseparable. They make up the "too-long-forgotten" *koinonia ethos* we need to rediscover.

Just as we are physically born into and nurtured by families, and just as we discover who we are in relationship with others, we grow as disciples, and discover our unique and special gifts in the context of *koinonia* - true community.

In the culture of Christ-centered communities, discipleship flourishes, gifts and ministries are distributed, and the world is "turned upside down." The transforming power of this ethos of belonging, growing and serving is seriously underestimated.

9 Lessons

The 9 weekly lessons that follow are meant to help us convert our *casual* Christian relationships into *committed* Christian relationships. Each Lesson will conclude with a Declaration - an Affirmation and a Commitment to the truths studied - and a Review Question or two.

By the time you finish the course, if you're not already part of a *koinonia group* (or whatever you want to call it), we hope you'll either join one or form one, and that you'll link with other similar groups for occasional larger gatherings. If you're a leader in your church, consider starting a *koinonia group* in your congregation.

These lessons grew out of a series of small group meetings in the Nashville area in the summer of 2011. We got started using this simple format:

> Scripture Reading & Listening - Worship - Short Talk - Discussion - Prayer

So... if you are ready for Lesson One, let's get started...

Lesson 1 - About Koinonia

What is Koinonia?

Koinonia is the Greek word that is often translated *fellowship* in Scripture. But it means much more than what we normally associate with the word *fellowship*. It means *sharing in common, participation with,* or *owning a share of common property with others,* and *in partnership with.*

Its first appearance in the New Testament is in Acts 2:42: "They devoted themselves to the apostles' teaching and to *koinonia* (the fellowship), to the breaking of bread and to prayer." And in verse 44, we are told "the believers were together and had everything in *koinos* (common)."

They devoted themselves to their life together. Their futures were intertwined with one another. The early church was much more communal than our Western churches are today. They took care of one another; they were partners together. We shouldn't idealize the early church, but, for sure, their lives were much more connected than we are used to. They were more "their brothers' keepers" than we are today, sharing responsibility together.

In some ways, with our heavy emphasis on personal autonomy, we have a cultural disadvantage in understanding the true nature of the church. The metaphors used in the New Testament to describe the people of God all imply a profound *interdependence*. Think about the interconnectedness implied in the metaphor of the Body of Christ (1 Cor. 12:27)... or of a temple being built together with other living stones (1 Peter 2:5; Eph. 2:22)... or of a household of faith (Eph. 2:19-22; 1 Tim. 3:15).

The idea of *koinonia* is rooted in the covenant nature of God's love (*hesed*). When we say "yes" to God's love, we become bonded with God and with the people of God. This bondedness is meant to be lived out in the context of families and communities.

In the KJV, *koinonia* sometimes refers to the covenant meal of the church, *communion*. For instance, in 1 Cor. 10:16: "The cup of blessing which we bless, is it not the communion (*koinonia*) of the blood of Christ? The bread which we break, is it not the communion (*koinonia*) of the body of Christ?" Breaking bread together is a profound statement of identification with one another just as we identify with

Christ. As we share the covenant meal, we should look around and realize *we're in this together!*

Responding to God's love, in Scripture, alway has 2 directions: vertical *and* horizontal - *Love God, and love your neighbor* (Mk. 12:30). "For anyone who does not love his brother, whom he has seen, cannot love God, whom he has not seen" (1 Jn. 4:20).

What Hinders Koinonia?

Here are just a few of the hinderances in experiencing koinonia:

Independence & Self-sufficiency;

Substituting Virtual Relationships for Face-to-Face Relationships;

The Fear of Being Known;

Schedules that Prioritize the Unimportant.

What else? _____ (If you're meeting with others, discuss.)

Finding the Few

What God expects us to become for the *many*, we learn among the *few*. Take, for instance, the 5th commandment - *Honor your father and mother*. God uses the family - the few - to teach us honor, which, of course, is a lesson he wants us to carry into all of life among the many.

Who are those *few* in your life? Who are those 6 or 8 people that God has set around you with whom you are to practice *koinonia?*

Think of it like the following picture: you are a living stone being built together with other living stones (Eph. 2:21-22; 1 Pet. 2:5). Who are those other *stones* that God is building you together with? Write their names down. Can you be so bold as to tell them how you see your relationship with them?

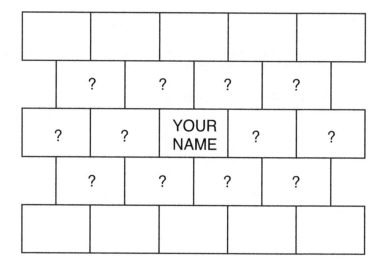

To help locate your *koinonia* brothers and sisters, ask these two questions:

1) For whom am I laying my life down, and who is laying his life down for me? ("This is how we know what love is: Jesus Christ laid down his life for us. And we ought to lay down our lives for our brothers." 1 John 3:16)

2) Whom do I *trust* to speak the truth to me in love, and who is it who *trusts* me to do the same with them? ("Speaking the truth in love, we will in all things grow up into him who is the Head, that is Christ." Eph. 4:15)

Declaration:

I acknowledge, Lord, that you want to build my life together with others. I renounce all attitudes or patterns of life that hinder that process. I choose interdependence over independence, and sacrifice and service over self-centeredness. I choose to be an agent, who, by your power, encourages koinonia, which is true community.

Review Questions:

(If you don't want to write in your book, you can download the Review Questions at **worshipschools.com/review-questions.pdf** to write your answers on.)

Q1.   What is *koinonia*? (See page 5)

A1.   _____

        _____

        _____

Q2.   How do I begin to experience *koinonia*? (See pages 6-7)

A2.   _____

        _____

        _____

(Write out your answers then compare with answers at the end of this booklet)

Lesson 2   - The Call to Discipleship

Believers or Disciples?

Koinonia and discipleship are very closely related. Before there can be koinonia, there must be a conversion of heart where we no longer live for ourselves, which is the essence of discipleship. And true community, where sacrificial love is practiced, strengthens us to walk as disciples. So *koinonia is the fruit of discipleship*, and *discipleship is sustained by koinonia*.

But, in the same way that the church has settled for "fellowship-lite," (instead of true *koinonia*), we often choose "discipleship-lite" instead of Biblical discipleship.

When Jesus called his disciples, he called them to a radical reorientation. We think we just need a *tune-up*; what we really need is an *overhaul*.

It is common to reduce the Christian life to proper *believing*. Becoming a disciple, however, is more about careful *obeying*.[1] What we are up against, in becoming a disciple, is a deeply rooted tendency to choose to go our own way rather than God's way. This is called *sin* - acting independently from God rather than in submission to God. "We all, like sheep, have gone astray, each of us has turned to his own way" (Is. 53:6). God's ways are very different from our ways (Is. 55:8). A disciple is someone who is learning to choose God's ways above his own ways.

Unfortunately, discipleship has come to be seen as an *add-on*, rather like adding fries to your order for a burger. Common thinking goes like this: *You have two choices - either one is OK: 1) you can become a regular believer, or, 2) if you really get serious, you can become a disciple.*

You've probably heard something like this: *some people know Jesus as Savior, others know him as Savior and Lord.* The only problem is, you don't find the "faith-without-discipleship" option offered anywhere in the New Testament.

What you *do* find is the comparison between being a *spiritual* Christian and a *worldly* (or *carnal*, KJV) Christian. Paul relates worldliness with

---

[1]   The word *believer* (or *believers*) is found in the N.T. 27 times; the word *disciple* (or *disciples*) is found 294 times.

spiritual infancy. "Brothers, I could not address you as spiritual but as worldly - mere infants in Christ" (1 Cor. 3:1).

Early in my Christian life, I saw the following three drawings. ["E" refers to Self (ego); the Cross signifies Jesus; the chair is the throne of a life; and the dots are the activities and interests of our lives.]

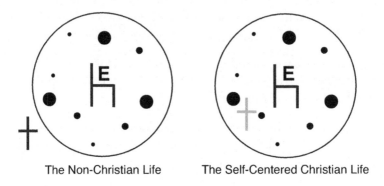

The Non-Christian Life   The Self-Centered Christian Life

The God-Centered Christian Life

In the first drawing, Jesus is outside the life and Self is in charge. This is the Non-Christian Life.

In the second drawing, Christ is in the life, but Self is still in charge, and, like the first, the activities and interests are out of order. This is a carnal or Self-Centered Christian Life.

In the third drawing, Christ is not only in the life, but ruling the life, and the activities and interests are ordered; there is peace. Self is still there, but not ruling. This is a God-Centered Life, or the life of someone surrendered to the Lord.

As a young Christian, I remember thinking *I want my life to be the third circle!*

When Jesus preached, he didn't make it easy to become a follower. *Unless you're willing to take up the cross, subject every relationship to me, and give up everything you have, you cannot be my disciple* (Luke 14:26-27; 33). Do you think we make it too easy?

Contrary to popular thinking, our salvation should *begin* with a commitment to the Lordship of Christ. According to Romans 10:9, salvation involves a confession of Jesus as our Lord. The Great Commission itself is as much about Discipleship as it is about Evangelism. *Go… make disciples… teaching them to obey everything I commanded you* (Mt. 28:19-20).

So what does it mean to live as disciples? What are the practices involved in the disciple's life? Let's consider these three essential practices: 1) living by the Word of God, 2) learning to walk in the Spirit, and 3) becoming accountable to others.

Living by the Word

In Jesus' words, "Man does not live on bread alone, but on every word that comes from the mouth of God" (Mt. 4:4). As bread, the Word of God keeps the people of God nourished and healthy. Without regular reading of Scripture, our independent minds tend to wander away from the truth. There is no discipleship, or true community, without the regular correction and inspiration from the Word of God.

That's why Paul required that the New Testament gatherings have public reading of the Scriptures (1 Tim. 4:13). Bonhoeffer, in *Life Together*, likewise insisted on the public reading of Scripture as fundamental to Christian communities.

And when we read the Scriptures publicly, we must learn to listen for how the Holy Spirit will apply his word to our lives. The interesting power of Scripture is that God can speak through the same reading to all the various needs of people at all the various levels of maturity.

In addition to public reading of Scripture is personal Bible reading. Consider using a plan like the One Year Bible that will have you not just reading your favorite passages but will broaden your exposure to all Scripture. Again, don't just read to *learn* facts, but to *hear* what the Lord wants to speak to you. As you read the Scriptures, constantly ask the Lord, "How does this apply to me?"

One of the most important principles of living by the Word is to share with others what you are learning. "Let the word of Christ dwell in you richly as you teach and admonish one another with all wisdom…" (Col. 3:16).

Learning to Walk in the Spirit

The disciple's motto is *not my will but yours be done* (Luke 22:42). That aspiration, however, is impossible to fulfill apart from God's empowering. That's where the Holy Spirit comes in.

Paul said it like this: "Those who live according to the sinful nature have their minds set on what that nature desires; but those who live in accordance with the Spirit have their minds set on what the Spirit desires" (Rom 8:5).

Growing as a disciple means growing in dependence upon the Holy Spirit, setting our minds on what pleases the Lord. Is that easy? No, it's not. Our hearts play tricks on us, deceiving us, rationalizing compromise, denying the convicting work of the Holy Spirit, even twisting the Word of God. And Satan himself is right there in our temptations, disguising himself as an angel of light, using all his treachery to try to move us away from a close communion with the Lord.

In those times, we need the Word of God, the Holy Spirit… and others!

Accountability to Others

Christ-followers need other Christ-followers to help them stay on track. Discipleship is not an individual sport. It requires a community. In community, we learn not only to be honest with God, but to be honest with others.

Here is an amazing passage from the apostle John: "…if we walk in the light (honesty), as he is in the light, we have fellowship (*koinonia*) with one another, and the blood of Jesus, his Son, purifies us from all sin. If we claim to be without sin, we deceive ourselves and the truth is not in us. If we confess our sins, he is faithful and just and will forgive us our sins and purify us from all unrighteousness" (1 John 1:7-9).

The cleansing of the blood of Jesus works in the context of *koinonia* where honesty is practiced. Confession of sin should be toward God and among those we trust. "Confess your sins to each other and pray for each other so that you may be healed" (James 5:16).

But how does accountability work? Just as God creates families to protect and care for children, God wants to give each of us a circle of relationships where we can learn honesty and accountability.[2]

Within the circle of relationships that God has for you, there will probably be someone who can serve as an older brother or mentor to you. When I came to Christ in college, the one who led me to the Lord became my first mentor. He and I were roommates for three years. After college, I was mentored by an established pastor. Since learning through those relationships, I have had the joy of mentoring others.

As we learn to submit to God's authority in a mentor or pastor, we will learn to submit to God's authority wherever it shows up. Paul tells the Ephesians to "submit to one another out of reverence for Christ" (Eph. 5:21). As one theologian said, "the same person will be sometimes 'subordinate' and sometimes 'superordinate' according to the gifts and graces being exercised."[3]

So a disciple is someone who lives to serve God and others above himself. The three practices of disciples are:

- They deeply value God's Word,

- They walk in dependence on the Holy Spirit; and

- They relate in honesty and accountability to others in the Body of Christ.

---

2   Technology has made it possible today to substitute virtual relationships for real, face-to-face relationships. Be careful of anything that allows you to have the illusion of relationships and yet maintain independence and preserve autonomy.

3   Colin Gunton, in *The Promise of Trinitarian Theology*. (Edinburgh: T & T Clark, 1997)

Declaration:

Lord, I pledge to take up my cross and follow you as a disciple, to allow you to rule my life as a king rules his subjects, to listen for and obey your Word to me through the Scriptures, to depend daily on the Holy Spirit, and to learn to walk in honesty and accountability with those who are becoming a spiritual community to me.

Review Question

Q3.   What does it mean to be a disciple of Jesus? (See Page 13)

A3.   _____

_____

_____

(Write out your answers then compare with answers at the end of this booklet)

Lesson 3 - What God Had in Mind When He Saved You

In the first two lessons, we learned about *koinonia* and *discipleship*. Now let's learn about growing in our gifts and callings - those special, Spirit-empowered abilities we receive to serve others, and those special assignments God gives us. We'll talk about the particular gifts of the Spirit later, but in this lesson, let's consider how to discover and engage in our gifts and callings.

My father, Gus Gustafson, wrote these words in his book, *Called to be a Layman*:

> "When we commit our lives to Jesus Christ, many radical changes take place, many new opportunities come our way. One of the most exciting is his call to purposeful living.
>
> Often we take this call for granted, even ignore it, going on with life as usual. But to do so is to miss out on the riches of kingdom living.
>
> In contrast to life as usual, Christ's urgent call is to a special assignment in kingdom building for each of us. We are the elect for that unique place in life. More than any other group, lay people are needed by God to advance his interests in fashioning the future of the world. For those of us who are ready to hear and are quick to respond, rewards are great and assured."

To go on with life as usual "is to miss out on the riches of kingdom living." My impression is that too many Christians do just that.

What did God have in mind when he saved you? Paul said, "I want to apprehend that for which also I am apprehended of Christ Jesus" (Phil. 3:12,KJV). To apprehend is to understand or perceive. A paraphrase could be "...that I may perceive the purpose for his saving me."

I can just imagine God watching Saul of Tarsus and thinking, "He's just the one to carry my name before the Gentiles and their kings." Before he called the brothers from Capernaum, I can imagine Jesus observing how they fished and thinking to himself, "They would be good at fishing for men." And regarding Abram, God was probably watching him and thinking, "He's just what I was looking for. I could bless nations through him and his descendants."

What was God thinking when he saw you? He had something in mind. What was it? And how can you better apprehend the details of that calling? How can you be fruitful in your calling?

Discovering what God had in mind for you starts with a major interruption. Life can't be the same! To Abram he said, "Leave home along with everything that is dear to you" (Gen. 12:1). The disciples left their nets. It begins with surrender - unreserved surrender.

Surrender to God

Think of it like this: one country (your life) has just been conquered by another (God's kingdom). The next step is a formal surrender.

In Luke 14, Jesus spells out the terms:

1. No Competing Relationships (vs. 26),

2. No Un-sacrificed Ambitions (vs. 27), and

3. No Unyielded Possessions (vs. 33).

All he asks is everything. "I tell you the truth, unless a kernel of wheat falls to the ground and dies, it remains only a single seed. But if it dies, it produces many seeds. The man who loves his life will lose it, while the man who hates his life in this world will keep it for eternal life" (John 12:24-25).

The following is from a book entitled *Surrender* by Nancy Leigh DeMoss:

> In 1951, there was an enterprising young man by the name of Bill, who was governed, as he said, by selfish goals and materialistic pursuits. Two years into marriage, he and his wife began to feel their hearts change. They were challenged by Jesus' words in Mark 8:34-35.
>
> *If any of you wants to be my follower... you must put aside your own pleasures, and shoulder your cross, and follow me closely. If you insist on saving your life, you will lose it. Only those who throw away their lives for my sake and for the sake of the Good News will ever know what it means to truly live. (TLB)*

One Sunday afternoon in the spring of 1951, as the young couple talked, they were gripped by the realization that knowing and serving the Lord Jesus was more important than any other pursuit in life. There in the living room of their home, they knelt together and prayed a simple, but heartfelt prayer:

Lord, we surrender our lives irrevocably to You and to do Your will.

We want to love and serve You with all of our hearts for the rest of our lives.

Bill describes one further step they took that day as an expression of their hearts' intent:

We actually wrote and signed a contract committing our whole lives to Him, relinquishing all of our rights, all of our possessions, everything we would ever own, giving to Him, our dear Lord and Master, everything. In the words of the Apostle Paul, (my wife) and I became that Sunday afternoon voluntary slaves of Jesus.

That *Bill* and his wife were *Bill & Vonette Bright*, who founded and led one of the largest Christian organizations in history with 70 different ministries, 26,000 full-time staff, and 126,000 trained volunteers, serving in 190 countries of the world.

Yet in spite of his many achievements, when Dr. Bright was diagnosed with terminal lung disease, he made it known that the only epitaph he and his wife wanted on their tombstone was "Slaves of Jesus Christ."

Someone once said that before we can know the details of God's will for our lives, he has us sign our name at the bottom of a blank contract, after which he fills in the details. Willingness to do his will precedes knowing what his will is. "Go to the land I will show you" (Gen. 12:1).

So the first step in knowing what God had in mind when he saved us is surrender.

Faithfulness

After our surrender, we begin to be exercised in faithfulness, in matters right in front of us. Many people think that we have to go to some far away place to prove our commitment. The Lord, however, will begin to train you right where you are.

In Luke 16, we learn where our callings begin:

1. Proving faithful in the little things (vs. 10),

2. Proving faithful in practical things, including money (vs. 11), and

3. Proving faithful in that which is another's (vs. 12).

This very extraordinary adventure begins with the very ordinary experiences of life - being faithful to God at your job, carrying out the trash, and paying the bills.

Give It Away

Whatever God gives you, find a way to share it. Share the experiences, resources and insights God gives you; you'll find there will be more. Give and you will have more to give. What do you have that you can share?

Look for needs in others that you are able to fulfill. It could be giving companionship to the elderly. It could simply be speaking encouragement to someone who is depressed, or maybe writing a letter to someone in jail. God is especially pleased when we give to those who can't repay us (Luke 14:12-14).

As you start giving to others in *general* ways, you'll begin to notice the *particular* ways God uses you. You may realize that you have a gift of encouraging, or leading, or teaching (etc.). (See Romans 12:6-8 for a partial listing of the various gifts God gives.) Your unique experiences and convictions will be noticeable in how you serve.

As you do these things, you are discovering your gifts and callings.

Acknowledging What You See in Others

Now, take notice of how God is using those around you. Acknowledge what you see - to them, and to others. For instance: *Have you noticed that when our group needs wisdom and direction that Fred is often the one God uses to provide us with leadership?* Or, *Time and again, when I run out of grace and compassion, you always seem to have a bountiful supply!*

In speaking up about these things, you'll inspire others to do the same. Discovering our gifts and callings is a group endeavor, like working together to put the pieces of a puzzle together. Sometimes, all it takes to activate a gift in someone is to publicly acknowledge it. Maybe you remember how someone told you that you were good at something, and how that motivated you to do it more? One of the benefits of finding *koinonia* is that it will help you know who you are in God, and how he wants to use you.

Declaration:

I choose to surrender to God unconditionally. I give up all rights of self determination, and boldly say, as Isaiah said, "Here am I, send me." As God helps me, I will learn faithfulness, practice giving away what he gives me, and pay attention to what God is doing in the lives of those around me, that I may fully discover those gifts he's given and engage in the calling he has for me, helping others do the same.

Review Question:

Q4. What are the main points to help you know what your gifts and callings are? (See Pages 16-19)

A4. _____

_____

_____

_____

(Write out your answer, then compare with answer at the end of this booklet.)

DEFINE Ethos

Lesson 4   - God's Plan for Growth

Fellowship

You may be thinking that _the koinonia ethos_ is just about your personal discipleship, and your small group of relationships. This week's lesson is meant to give us a bigger picture - to help us see that _koinonia_, when practiced, has the potential to powerfully transform cultures - the church's and even the world's!

Years ago, I had a song recorded whose words went like this:

> _There will never be an end of his ever-increasing kingdom,_
> _There will always be an ever-increasing peace._
> _When the government shall be upon his shoulders,_
> _There will never be an end, there will never be an end,_
> _There will always be an ever-increasing kingdom._
>
> _Thine is the Kingdom (1991)_

The essential idea of the song, based on Isaiah 9:6-7, is that there can simultaneously be unending growth and increasing peace if we allow him to shoulder the kingdom, instead of us. That is what the doctrine of the Headship of Christ is about - Christ being the presiding king of his kingdom, and not us! This is what we pray in the Lord's prayer when we say, "Yours is the kingdom." _Toni Cassidy praying in front_

give me what you want me to have

Upon His Shoulders

Howard Snyder writes this in _The Community of the King_[4]:

> There is something spontaneous about genuine church growth. Church growth throughout history has shown this repeatedly. Normal growth does not depend upon successful techniques or programs, though planning has its place. Rather, growth is the normal consequence of spiritual life. What is alive grows. Normal church growth is spontaneous in the sense that the nature of the church is to grow - spiritually, numerically and in cultural impact...

---

[4]   © 1977 & 2004, IVP Academic (Downers Grove, IL)

> Roland Allen was right to speak of "the spontaneous expansion of the church."[5]

> Church growth is not a matter of bringing to the church that which is necessary for growth, for if Christ is there through the Holy Spirit, the seeds of growth are already present. Rather, church growth is a matter of removing hindrances to growth. The church will naturally grow if not limited by unbiblical barriers."

We've already talked about the importance of "speaking the truth in love" and of each one of us learning to give to others what God has given us ("that which each part supplies"). But here is the radical implication of these two practices: As we learn *truth speaking* in the context of *koinonia,* and each member doing its part, we are actually discovering the biblical secret of growing the church.

According to Ephesian 4:12-16, God gave spiritual leaders...

> ...to prepare God's people for works of service, so that the body of Christ may be built up until we all reach unity in the faith and in the knowledge of the Son of God and become mature, attaining to the whole measure of the fullness of Christ.
> Then we will no longer be infants, tossed back and forth by the waves, and blown here and there by every wind of teaching and by the cunning and craftiness of men in their deceitful scheming. Instead, speaking the truth in love, we will in all things grow up into him who is the Head, that is, Christ. From him the whole body, joined and held together by every supporting ligament, grows and builds itself up in love, as each part does its work." (Eph. 4:12-16.)

Wow! Reaching unity regarding faith and knowledge of Jesus, and attaining to the "whole measure of the fullness of Christ"! Protection

---

[5]   Roland Allen (1868-1947) wrote *The Spontaneous Expansion of the Christian Church* in 1927. It was about removing barriers to the growth of the kingdom. As an Anglican missionary in China and later Africa, he pleaded for his church's leadership to trust the work of the Holy Spirit in the emerging indigenous church leaders in mission churches. Today Allen is honored with a feast day (June 8) on the Episcopal Church (USA)'s liturgical calendar.

from deception! The body of Christ builds itself up in love! "We will in all things grow up into him who is the Head"!

There are so many plans and programs and approaches that promise church growth. Mega-church experts who lead thousands are eager to tell us how it's done. But are they as effective as the simple methods Paul described in Ephesians 4?

To the extent that the members of a fellowship are being trained for works of service, and to the extent that those members are learning *truth speaking* with one another, to that extent will they mature, growing up into Christ's active leadership in their lives. You could call this the *discipleship-koinonia approach* to growing churches.

The opposite is also true: to the extent that we are not being prepared for service to others, and to the extent that we are not practicing honest, sacrificial relationships with one another, to that extent are we guaranteeing life-long spiritual infancy and vulnerability to deception. You could call this the *growth-without-discipleship approach*.

In the early 1950's, when foreign mission agencies were forced out of China because of the Communist takeover, the Chinese church began to grow at an astounding rate. How did it happen? Small groups had to become the fundamental (not incidental) context of Christian fellowship, and disciples made disciples who made disciples. And all this happened without outside funding, church buildings or seminary-trained leaders. They had to learn dependence on the Holy Spirit.

With all of our advantages in the West, we are usually not as effective. But we could be, by returning to the ethos of *koinonia* and discipleship.

Understanding the New Covenant

Why is this *koinonia ethos* effective in creating growth? I believe it is because it's the ethos of the New Covenant itself.

Hear me out. Jeremiah prophesied that there would one day be a New Covenant which would contrast with what we now call the Old Covenant. Our Bibles are divided into these two covenants or "testaments." A covenant is a legal description defining how two parties relate to each other.

Jeremiah said in chapter 31, verse 31, that, in this coming New Covenant, God would put his law in the minds and hearts of his people. In the New Covenant, we are to have an internal, rather than external, motivation to obey God.

Paul, in 2 Corinthians 3:7-8, contrasts the Old Covenant law with the "ministry of the Spirit." When we come to Jesus and become a Christian, we meet the one whom John the Baptist introduced to the world as the one who "will baptize you with the Holy Spirit" (Mark 1:7-8.) When Jesus baptizes us with the Holy Spirit, we are immersed in and saturated with the Holy Spirit. Jesus told his disciples that the Holy Spirit would be in them and lead them "into all truth" (John 14:16-17, 16:13).

The Holy Spirit is not optional for Christians. He is the one who administrates the New Covenant. He is one who convicts us of sin. The gifts God gives us are given "by the Spirit" (1 Corinthians 12:4-11). The character God wants us to acquire is called "the fruit of the Spirit" (Galatians 5:22-23).

So the New Covenant is administered by the Holy Spirit. How does this relate to discipleship?

For three years, Jesus trained his disciples, and then said, "It is for your good that I am going away. Unless I go away the Counselor will not come to you" (John 16:7). The goal of discipleship is to bring a believer into a vital relationship with the Holy Spirit who will then guide him into all truth. Then the mentor "goes away." Maybe not physically, but he releases the one trained to go train others. Every parent of adult children knows about this process, when you release your child from your authority to go and start his own household.

The relationship does not end, but it does change. Leadership becomes more a matter of influence than of management. Those trained by this kind of discipleship will find themselves working together with others like a colony of ants in which there is some kind of invisible leadership that directs and coordinates the activity. It's the mind of Christ!

I'm fascinated by the organization of Alcoholics Anonymous. Millions of people have overcome serious addictions by their methods. AA grows by *attraction*, rather than *promotion*. Participation requires truth telling, and everyone has a sponsor or host, someone who is a little further along than they are. I think the reason it has become a "church substitute" for some is that AA has discovered neglected practices that once belonged to the church.

Of particular interest is that this kind of organization is governed by an ethos, and it has the potential to grow spontaneously as the ethos is constantly reinforced. In that respect, it's the same kind of organization the New Covenant will produce.

A Meeting, a Mission and a Community

I live in Nashville where there are 3 or 4 music studios on every block. A mixing board is the hardware you use to mix the various tracks that go into making a recording. Sliders move the presence of a particular track in the mix up or down. Let's use that analogy to think of the church.

The church is a *Meeting*, or a gathering. When we say we're going to church, this is what we're thinking, we're going to a *Meeting*. The church is also a *Mission*. Our *Mission* to take the good news of Jesus and his kingdom to the world, and to stand for his truth in the world. The church is also a *Community*, a family, a household of faith.

Generally, we do *Meetings* pretty well. We pour a lot of energy into planning and executing church *Meetings*. Between 1 to 10, let's say we're at about 8 or 9 in doing *Meetings*. *Missions*? Some churches are better than others, but let's say generally we're at about 6 or 7.

But *Community*? Usually not good at all. Maybe a 2 at best. John Stott said that one of the reasons for the effectiveness of cults is that they do a better job of providing community.[6]   ⌐ Remnant

In emphasizing the recovery of *koinonia*, we're not saying that the church is not a *Meeting* or a *Mission*. But we are saying that we have prioritized those aspects of being the church to the neglect of *Community*. Back to the analogy of the mixing board.

---

[6]   *The Contemporary Christian,* John Stott (InterVarsity Press, 1992)

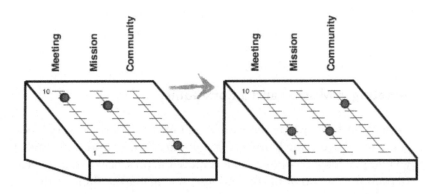

The drawing on the left is a picture of great *Meetings* & activity in *Mission*, but a very low level of *koinonia*. We've got to get *Community* up "in the mix" even if it means dropping down *Meetings* and *Mission* - see the drawing on the right. We may discover, as we move from the drawing on the left to the one on the right, that we become more effective in *Mission* and more genuine in our *Meetings*.

In the mid-1700's, during the Wesleyan revival in England, large groups of new converts formed. These were called *Societies*. They were similar to our congregations today. Then, as a result of a small group experiment in Bristol, the *Societies* were broken down into *Classes*. In the *Classes*, 12 people met weekly with a Class Leader for pastoral care, examination, encouragement and exhortation. According to Wesley, "Many now happily experienced that Christian fellowship of which they had not so much as an idea before. They began to 'bear one another's burdens,' and naturally to 'care for each other.' As they had daily a more intimate acquaintance with, so they had a more endeared affection for each other."[7]

The *Classes* became the centerpiece of Methodism for the next 100 years, impacting England and the United States in incredible ways!

What Could Happen?

In summary, God's plan for growth involves, on our part, learning the simple practices of truth speaking, growing into Christ's headship and every member engaging in his ministry or service. We're calling this the *discipleship-koinonia approach* to growth. Although this approach involves a significant shift of priorities - from understanding the church only as a

---

[7]   *The Journal of John Wesley*. February, 1742

How do we deal with those who are not "known" Popes - Albrect's

e ccc

meeting or a *mission*, to seeing it as a vital *community* of relationships - it holds tremendous promise of unending, spontaneous growth.

What could happen if your small group of friends began to walk even more closely together, to share one anothers' dreams, to listen together to God's voice, and, empowered by the Holy Spirit, to serve one another and those around them?

Could that ethos of hearing and obeying God together truly radiate out to affect the world you live in? Could that group of friends, like Jesus', grow and multiply like those early small fellowships in the New Testament, until, like yeast leavening the whole loaf, a whole generation is affected? Could a contagion like that begin in our day?

I say, "Let's see if it could!"

Read

Declaration:

Together we declare that we are hungry to be part of something that grows of itself. We long to see the spontaneous expansion of the church. So we invite the Holy Spirit to write God's laws in our hearts and minds, and to lead us into all truth. We welcome the training he has in mind for us so that we can be prepared to train others as we grow up into Christ's active Headship of our lives together.

Review Questions:

Q5.   What is the doctrine of the Headship of Christ? (See page 21)

A5.   _____

_____

_____

Q6.   What is the secret of church growth found in Ephesians 4:15-16? (See page 22-23)

A6.   _____

         _____

         _____

(Write out your answers then compare with answers at the end of this booklet)

Lesson 5 - What Are Your Gifts and Callings?

Let's review. The *koinonia ethos* is about *community*, *discipleship* and *service to others*. In Lesson 1, we learned that God has in mind for us a level of fellowship with one another that is rarely experienced among Christians. We're calling it *koinonia*. It happens when we learn to truly lay our lives down for one another.

Discipleship was the focus in Lesson 2. Discipleship involves a radical reorientation where we learn to live as God-centered people rather than self-centered. As disciples, we acquire the habits of listening to and obeying God's Word, depending on the Holy Spirit and walking in honesty and accountability with God's people.

Lesson 3 was about taking the first steps in discovering God's special assignments for our lives. These steps include surrender to God's will, faithfulness, giving away what God gives us, and discerning our gifts through our community relationships.

Then, in Lesson 4, we began to get the vision of how the church grows spontaneously as we learn the *koinonia ethos*. The simple practices of truth speaking and equipping one another cause us to grow up into the Headship of Christ, and the body grows and builds itself up as every part does its work.

Now, in Lesson 5, we want to build on what we began in Lesson 3 in understanding our gifts and callings. Let's examine the fascinating study of *charisma* - the gifts of the Spirit - and how important they are in serving others.

What's the Big Fuss?

In some circles, the subject of spiritual gifts creates controversy. Some say that the gifts died out at the end of the New Testament era, and others narrowly define the gifts only to include their favorite few, and then, make them out to be badges of distinction and even superiority. Let's steer clear of both errors.

Howard Snyder, in *Community of the King*, has these words of wisdom:

> Fellowship and community life are necessary within
> the Church in order to equip Christians for their various
> kinds of witness and service. In one way or another every

Christian is a witness in the world and must share his faith. But he can be an effective witness only as he experiences the enabling common life of the Church. And this common life is truly enabling only as the community becomes, through the indwelling of Christ and the exercise of spiritual gifts, the *koinonia* of the Holy Spirit.

The gifts of the Spirit in the Christian community must be seen not as spiritual fringe benefits but as completely central to the life, experience and functioning of the Christian community...

The basic question is not whether specific spiritual gifts, such as those of apostle, prophet or tongues-speaking, are valid today. The question is whether the Spirit still "gives gifts to men," and the answer is *yes*. Precisely which gifts he gives in any particular age is God's prerogative, and we should not prejudge God. Interpretations as to specific gifts may vary. But we have no biblical warrant to restrict the *chasimata* to the early church nor to ban any specific gift today. Arguments against gifts generally arise from secondary, not biblical, considerations and a fear of excesses or abuses.

The gifts are given to help us serve others. There's no basis for pride in that. Think of it like this. You just got a new job, but you don't have the skills to carry out some of the responsibilities your new job requires. Not to worry, your employer provides you with the tools to do what you are asked to do. That's what God does for us with these gifts. They are tools given to help us do our job.

Sometimes a word accrues so much baggage that it is no longer useful. It either needs to be discarded or redefined. The word *charismatic* is an example. But before we discard it, let's see if we can understand, from a Biblical perspective, what's behind it.

The Greek word for a spiritual gift is *charisma*. It is closely related to the Greek word *charis*, which means *grace* or *gift*. Think of a spiritual gift (*charisma*) as a little package of Spirit-charged grace (*charis*) given by God to help you serve others.

"Each one should use whatever gift (*charisma*) he has received to serve others, faithfully administering God's grace (*charis*) in its various forms. If anyone speaks, he should do it as one speaking the very words of God. If anyone serves, he should do it with the strength God provides, so that in all things God may be praised through Jesus Christ." 1 Peter 4:10-11.

Each one should use whatever form of God's grace has been given him to serve others. Seems pretty basic, doesn't it? But what are these "various forms" of God's grace?

There are several lists of spiritual gifts in the Scripture - 1 Corinthians 12 and Romans 12, for instance. None of the lists are meant to be comprehensive. In fact, the first thing we learn about the gifts in 1 Corinthians 12 is that there is great variety among the gifts and operations of the Spirit (vs. 4-6). Some of the listed gifts in these two passages are healing, miracles, faith, word of wisdom, word of knowledge, prophecy, leadership, encouragement, teaching, service, generosity, and showing mercy.

By the way, since this list includes encouragement, service and generosity, we should hope the charismatic gifts haven't died out. If they have, we're in big trouble! Maybe to help restore the word *charismatic* to its real meaning, next time you catch someone exercising the gifts of service or encouragement, remind them that they are *charismatic*.

It could be that the disagreements about the contemporary use of the gifts of the Spirit are more attitudinal than theological. They simply reveal differences in how we express spirituality. Different groups do go at it differently. They have different governing mindsets. For instance, Paul compared the Jews, who measured spirituality by miraculous signs, and Greeks, who measured spirituality by wisdom (see 1 Cor. 1:22). They had two different sets of spiritual priorities. Could it be we have similar differences today among God's people?

Maybe it would help if we divided the gifts into these two categories: the *daily* and the *dramatic*. The *daily* gifts of the Spirit go almost unnoticed - encouragement and leadership, for example; the *dramatic* are unusual and out of the ordinary - tongues and prophecy, for instance. Some of us may be wired with a spirituality that needs more drama, and thus we really like the *dramatic* gifts. Others of us have a different spiritual metabolism and latch on to the *daily* gifts.

These preferences are not bad, and probably serve as a balance to each other. But, just as Paul said Christ was bigger than either the Jewish or Greek spiritualities ("Christ is the power of God and the wisdom of God," 1 Cor. 1:24), God will challenge our preferences when it comes to the gifts. Don't you know God just loved surprising the Greeks with miraculous signs, and the Jews with wisdom and insight. Don't be surprised that he challenges you on your personal preferences too!

God challenged me one time. Years ago, I was walking down the street with a Muslim friend, Arbi Omar from Tripoli. A strange idea come into my mind: sing a song to him in an unknown language! I asked him, "Arbi, have you ever heard this song?" and began singing an unknown melody in an unknown language. He turned to me with a startled look. "Where did you learn that song?" It turned out, I was not only singing a song in his language, I was singing a song that was unique to his own people in North Africa. Nothing else would have gotten through to him like that!

I would put that in the *dramatic* category! But, you know, there are other spiritual gifts I admire even more. In 1988, I had the opportunity of interviewing Mother Theresa in Calcutta, India. I saw in her, and throughout her Missionaries of Charity organization, gifts of service that were awesome in power in bringing Jesus to one of the most needy cities in the world. She was a modern-day Dorcas, who, the Bible says, "was always doing good and helping the poor" (Acts 9:36). Truly, the gifts of the Spirit have not died out!

Paul tells us two important things about the gifts: 1) Don't be ignorant of them, and 2) eagerly desire them (1 Cor. 12:1, 31)!

Shouldn't we all have the attitude that says to God "Do whatever you want. We are your servants!" (We're surrendered, remember? Lesson 3.)

Native Gifts or Spiritual?

Some who have taught on the spiritual gifts have made the point that spiritual gifts have very little correlation to the *natural* gifts that we had before we came to Christ. But I would have to say that, looking back, I can see God was working in my life in many ways before I ever acknowledged him. The distinction should be between gifts being empowered by God's Holy Spirit instead of by our own human energy, rather than between "pre" or "post" conversion.

Paul had a gift of determined leadership before he came to Christ that became empowered and directed by the Holy Spirit after he came to Christ. There are probably some inclinations (not all) that you had before your conversion that God will resurrect and use in your new life with him.

Moved with Compassion

One of the best ways to discover how the Holy Spirit will work in you and through you is to watch for when compassion springs up in you. Here's how I learned this. I am a teacher, and I find myself moved with compassion when I see the people of God languishing because of a lack of wisdom or knowledge. Furthermore, there are certain things that, when I speak on them, I become aware that they are very fitting for the hearers. I know, because I feel a rush of compassion to the point where I almost can't talk. I have learned that God is at work in those special times.

Years ago, I heard one of the spiritual fathers in Nashville, Don Finto, explain this. He noted that before many miracles Jesus performed, he was "moved with compassion." (For example: "When Jesus landed and saw a large crowd, he had compassion on them and healed their sick." Mt. 14:14. See also Matt. 15:32, 20:34; Mk. 1:41; 6:34).

The original meaning of this phrase for *having compassion* was that he was moved in *the bowels of mercy.* (For instance, compare Col. 3:12 in the KJV - *bowels of mercies* - with the NIV - *compassion.*) The Greek word here is *splanchna.* It's probably similar to what we mean when we say in "pit of our stomach." It refers to a deep-seated, visceral kind of spiritual emotion that seems to come from our lower abdomen, the same place from which laughter and certain fears well up. When we see this at work in someone's life, my wife and I say, "Their *splanchna* is going off." Your sphere of ministry to others will be closely related to the way compassion moves in you.

Insight

Another indicator of your gifting is where you find that you have insight into certain matters, or implicit faith or confidence about something. You'll see certain tasks, challenges or needs differently than others. David truly couldn't understand why everyone else was afraid of Goliath. Turns out, he was operating in his gift!

Do you remember the movie *Chariots of Fire?* In it, Eric Liddell, the Olympic runner told his missionary sister, "God made me fast, and when I run I feel his pleasure." How has God made you? How has he gifted you?

Two Assignments:

>   1) Write down something about how God works through you.

>   2) Write down a gift that you desire God to give you.

Declaration: We affirm the reality and the necessity of the various gifts God has to give us to help us in our service to others. We eagerly invite the Lord to impart to our hearts and lives these Spirit-charged packages of God's grace.

Review Question:

>   Q7.   Why were the gifts of the Spirit given to the church? (See page 30)

>   A7.   _____

>   _____

>   _____

(Write out your answers then compare with answers at the end of this booklet)

Lesson 6 - Beyond Small Groups - Networking Koinonia

Community matters. That's about like saying oxygen matters. As our lungs require air, so our souls require what only community provides. We were designed by our Trinitarian God (who is himself a group of three persons in profound relationship with each other) to live in relationship...

The future of the church depends on whether it develops true community. We can get by for a while on size, skilled communication, and programs to meet every need, but unless we sense that we belong to each other, with masks off, the vibrant church of today will become the powerless church of tomorrow. Stale, irrelevant, a place of pretense where sufferers suffer alone, where pressures generate conformity rather than the Spirit-creating life - that's where the church is headed unless it focuses on community.[8]

I have been asked if the term I'm using - *koinonia groups* - is just another phrase for small groups, or maybe *house churches*. I look at both the small group movement and the house church movement favorably. In most cases, they are getting us closer to experiencing community. But, if your small group only meets once or twice a month, and, if that's the only occasion of being together, it's unlikely that true community is happening.

What constitutes a *koinonia group* is not where it meets. It could be in a home, but it could also be at a coffee shop, a church fellowship hall or a rented meeting room. It's the nature of the relationships within the group that distinguishes it. Is there sacrificial love, shared responsibility for one another, and common purpose?

---

[8]   Larry Crabb, in the foreword to Randy Frazee's *The Connecting Church* - Zondervan, 2001

What we're going to look at, in Lesson 6 is how to move beyond small groups to authentic community[9]. We're also going to discuss how vital it is that these mini-communities (*koinonia groups*) connect with the larger body of Christ.

Beyond Small Groups

According to George Gallup, Jr., "40 percent of U.S. adults are involved in small groups of some sort that meet on a regular basis and include nurture and sharing. Six in ten of these groups are connected with a faith community." How is it, then, that many sociologists have concluded that Americans are among the loneliest people in the world[10]?

In *The Connecting Church* (which I highly recommend), Randy Frazee tells the story of a leadership retreat where the subject of small groups came up. When the discussion got honest, they discovered that there was a high level of frustration with their small group experience. Although small groups were a priority in their church, there was a sense of obligation toward them, rather than heartfelt enthusiasm. In many cases, people were just attending the small groups, but not really engaging, in much the same way many people attend a weekly congregational service.

That led Frazee to study of the elements of cohesive communities, including the Amish, Israeli kibbutzim, certain military units, and even American gangs. He also documented the deep-seated nature of the sociological issues that prevent the experience of genuine community.

Common Purpose, Common Place & Common Possessions

He found three broad categories of essential elements that make up cohesive communities: 1) Common Purpose, 2) Common Place, and 3) Common Possessions. Bonding takes place when our individual plans and purposes are subjected to an overarching purpose, when we live our lives in close proximity with one another[11], and when we are willing to share our resources with others.

---

[9] I'm borrowing from the byline of Frazee's *The Connecting Church*, which is "Beyond Small Groups to Authentic Community."

[10] George Gallup, Jr., *The People's Religion* (Macmillan, 1989)

[11] "Better a neighbor nearby than a brother far away" (Prov. 27:10).

According to Frazee's study, *common purpose* is found in communities where there are these ingredients: respect for the authority structure, shared beliefs and values, shared traditions, accepted standards and a common mission.

Finding *common place* refers to spending time together. In the communities he studied, Frazee found these characteristics: the members saw each other with *frequency*, they lived close by each other (*proximity*), they made themselves available to the others (*availability*), their meetings were not just planned (*spontaneity*), and they shared *common meals*.

Regarding *common possessions*, don't get scared. We're not all going to join a commune. The heart of a disciple toward things is that he is a steward, not an owner, of what God entrusts to us. There should be a point in the life of every Christian where we give up all rights to our possessions (Luke 14:33), after which God then will give wisdom to know how to manage the possessions that no longer belong to us. There are times in history where God seems to have required dramatic abandonment of possessions with individuals and groups. Take for instance the early church (Acts 2:44-45), Francis of Assisi, Count von Zinzendorf,[12] and the first few years of the Plymouth Colony.[13]

In becoming true Christian communities, there is some important thinking we need to do regarding attitudes toward personal responsibility and shared responsibility. Galatians 6:2 challenges us to *bear one another's burdens*, while Galatians 6:5 says that *each one should bear his own load*. The two potential problems are: 1) people who don't want to do their part and are happy for others to take care of them, and 2) people who are doing their part but are unwilling to share with those in need.[14] The Holy Spirit may simultaneously challenge one person toward greater personal responsibility, and another person to greater generosity. We should all remember, too, that there are seasons of

---

[12]   Zinzendorf, who lived in Germany from 1700 to 1760, offered asylum on his estate for persecuted Moravian believers. The community that grew out of this generosity became known as Herrnhut.

[13]   After experimenting with communal property for a couple of years, the leaders at Plymouth allotted private land plots, after which there was a marked increase of productivity.

[14]   You can see how these two challenges in forming community are also challenges that we face at a national, political level.

difficulty, as well as seasons of prosperity, that all of us will face. Be there for one another, no matter the season.

Generally, the long-term principle of *common possessions* is this: <u>Be personally responsible for entrusted possessions with an attitude of generosity toward those in need, especially for those in the household of faith</u>.[15] Or simply, *be responsible and generous with what God entrusts to you.*

To be realistic, the culture of independence is firmly entrenched all around us.[16] Many of us simply will never trade in our autonomy for community. Oh, we'll read books about it, we'll talk about it. We will even secretly admire those who experience it, but still lack the courage to move toward *common purpose, common place and common possessions* with those God has put in our lives for *koinonia.*

Even small groups or house churches may never challenge our disconnectedness. Princeton's Robert Wuthnow studied small groups and concluded that they mainly "provide occasions for individuals to focus on themselves in the presence of others. The social contract binding members together asserts only the weakest of obligations. Come if you have time... Never criticize. Leave quietly if you become dissatisfied."[17]

From Casual Relationships to Committed

What practical steps can we take to convert our casual Christian relationships into committed Christian relationships? Remember the picture of the other living stones that surround you, that set of six or eight relationship that are already in your life? Adjust your schedule so that you see each one of them at least once or twice a week. Do things together. Have them over for meals. Learn of what they're going through, where they're headed. Spend time with them. Pray for them!

If appropriate, be so bold as to suggest meeting together on a weekly basis with some of them. Read Scripture together, listen for what God says to you together. Talk about what the will of God might be for each

---

[15]   See 2 Cor. 9:11 & Gal. 6:10 - made rich for the purpose of generosity, toward all men, especially the household of faith.

[16]   Entrenched = "firmly established and difficult or unlikely to change"

[17]   Quoted by John L. Locke in *The De-Voicing of Society, Why We Don't Talk to Each Other Any More* (New York, Simon and Schuster, 1998).

other. Encourage each other. Be discipled and make disciples. Get to know your friends' friends. Welcome them to join you. The adventure unfolds!

Connecting Groups

Wayne Meeks, a historian who researched the social world of the first-century church, noted this: "One peculiar thing about early Christianity was the way in which the intimate, close-knit life of the local groups was seen to be simultaneously part of a much larger, indeed ultimately worldwide, movement or entity."[18]

Without connection to other groups, a small group or small church can become insular. Do you remember in Lesson 4, we talked about how John Wesley organized the early Methodists into Societies and Classes? The Societies were similar to our congregations and the Classes, to what we're calling *koinonia groups*. In their case, they started with Societies, and developed Classes. It can work the other way too, where we start with spiritual households and find ways to integrate into a network of other similar groups.

To connect groups, leaders of groups need to meet with leaders of other groups. As this happens, plan joint meetings. I think a good pattern is <u>weekly fellowship group meetings, and monthly joint meetings of fellowship groups</u>. Think of the Biblical pattern of families, clans, tribes and the nation. Most of the day-to-day activities happened at the family and clan level, but there were times when there were larger activities that involved the tribes and the nation.

Ideally, *koinonia groups* would connect with other groups to form congregations, and congregations would connect with other congregations in a local area to be part of the larger church in the city or locality. If you are already connected to a congregation - maybe you are its pastor - talk to your leaders about forming *koinonia groups* within your congregation. The critical issue will be this: will these groups be allowed to be fundamental in importance rather than incidental?

---

[18]   Wayne A. Meeks, *The First Urban Christians: The Social World of the Apostle Paul* (New Haven, CT, Yale University Press, 1983) 105.

The Analogy of the Internet

In distinguishing between *koinonia* groups and other small group models, I'm not trying to be nitpicky. I'm trying to identify and discover the basic building block of kingdom life. The basic unit used to be understood as the congregation, and more recently, the small group. Now we're learning about *koinonia*.

What we're discovering is that church is not primarily a meeting we attend, but a network of relationships in which we participate. Said in another way: *the church, the body of Christ, is essentially a network of relationships of which the basic unit is a family-like group where koinonia is practiced.*

Some people think that *networks* are elusive, whereas *organizations* are manageable and solid. Not necessarily. One of the best analogies of this is the internet, which is essentially a network. Websites are little hubs of activity and information that are linked with other similar hubs. The resulting global network, which has so dramatically changed the world, was only a theoretical possibility until 1982 when the Internet Protocol Suite (TCP/IP) was standardized and the concept of a world-wide network of fully interconnected TCP/IP networks called the Internet was introduced.

Once we get to the fundamentals of the church's atomic structure - which I believe are *koinonia*, *discipleship* and *service* under the active headship of Christ - and see how those basic units of fellowship relate with others, the potential for networks of relationships to emerge is awesome! That's what the Chinese church discovered; and the early Methodists; and the early church, itself. And who knows, maybe that's what spiritual households will discover in America or other countries?

Declaration: We declare that the church is a network of relationships under Christ, and we declare that, by the power of the Holy Spirit, we will actively participate in the relationships the Lord has created around us for his glory!

Review Question:

Q8.   What are the three elements that make small groups
into communities? Explain each. (See page 36-38)

A8.   _____

_____

_____

_____

(Write out your answers then compare with answers at the end of
this booklet)

Lesson 7   - Healing Communities

Community, *discipleship* and *service to others* - not only are these the right things to be involved with, but as we participate, we, and others, experience healing.

In 1997, Larry Crabb wrote *Connecting*[19]. Here are some excerpts from his Introduction. They are very pertinent for those of us wanting to experience *koinonia*.

> Maybe "going to church," more than anything else, means relating to several people in your life differently. *Maybe the center of Christian community is connecting with a few...*
>
> I am now working toward the day when communities of God's people, ordinary Christians, whose lives regularly intersect, will accomplish most of the good that we now depend on mental health professionals to provide...
>
> Imagine what could happen if God were to place within his people intangible nutrients that had the power to both prevent and reverse soul disease, and then told us to share those nutrients with each other in a special kind of intimate relating called connection... Like spiritual gifts, these nutrients only nourish our own souls as we give them away for the blessing of others...
>
> I have been captured by the idea that God has placed extraordinary resources within us that have the power to heal us and our relationships...
>
> I envision the church as people who are connected in small healing communities, connected by what they give to each other. Perhaps they gather with other little communities in larger groups to celebrate the life they share and be instructed in that life and then go out to connect even more deeply and invite others to enjoy the same intimacy...
>
> (Community has) the potential to liberate, strengthen, encourage... and to touch the deepest, deadest, most terrifying parts of people's souls with resurrection power...

---

[19]   Word Publishing, 1997, Nashville, TN

Beneath what our culture calls psychological disorder is a soul crying out for what only community can provide... Damaged psyches aren't the problem. The problem beneath the struggles is a disconnected soul...

It's about time to go beneath the moralism that assumes the church is done when it instructs people in biblical principles and then exhorts them to do right. It's about time to find a better way to help each other when we struggle than the way of our therapeutic culture, which looks beneath every troublesome emotion or behavior pattern to find a psychological disorder that needs repair...

I don't want to focus on the hard things, the ugly things, the awful things. I don't want to gloss over them... but I do want us to look beneath all that is difficult and see the miracle God has wrought in our hearts.

I want us to see that he has placed powerful urges to do good in the deepest recesses of our regenerated hearts. That's what the New Covenant is all about...

I want us to relate to one another, not as moralist to sinner or therapist to patient, but as saint to saint... with the confidence that we can help each other believe that, by the grace of God, there is something good beneath the mess...

This... is a call to healing relationships... a call away from the assumption that professional training equips people better than godliness to speak powerfully into people's lives...

We cannot become all we could be without the love, wisdom, and feedback of others. I am writing to anyone who yearns to escape the miseries of loneliness and meaningless existence by richly connecting with at least a few other people...

The greatest need in modern civilization is the development of communities.

How Can We Become Healing Communities?

Think about your little group, those few individuals with whom God is knitting your heart and life. Ask these questions:

1. How much of my story do they know? How much of their stories do I know?

2. Would I drop what I'm doing to help them if they asked?

3. Have we ever shared a meal at one of our homes?

4. Do I know their children's names? Do I know anything about their parents?

5. Is there enough trust in these relationships that I could share a difficult struggle with them and not fear their rejection or misunderstanding?

6. Do they encourage me to hear and obey God? Do I encourage them in the same way?

Speaking the Truth

We've talked about the importance of speaking the truth with one another. Let's look at some of the inner workings of this vital, soul-nourishing, life-giving practice.

For many people, "speaking the truth in love" surprisingly has a negative connotation. They're expecting the hammer to fall. Something like, "Brother, I love you, but…" And then comes the dreaded rebuke. There are certainly times when a rebuke is necessary, but speaking the truth in love is so much more than just that.

Speaking the truth begins with respect. That other person is created in the image of God. Admire them for that. Don't measure their value by what you can gain from the relationship. Love means that you are there to build them up. Conversation is not so you can impress them with what you know or gain ascendency over them. It is not so that you can fix them, change them or even convert them. It is to *edify* them. "Encourage one another and build each other up" (1 Thess. 5:11).

We all tend to tip-toe cautiously toward transparency. But when people sense respect, it will be more natural for the conversation to go beyond surface things.

Next, speaking the truth requires that we listen. Listen to, and in behalf of, the other person. Practice this: "Quick to listen, slow to speak and slow to become angry" (James 1:19). "He who answers before listening - that is his folly and his shame" (Prov. 18:13).

Listen carefully to them, in the same manner you would like others listen to you. Listen to what *they* say, and listen to what *God* is saying. Listen beyond just what their words say.

Don't quickly conclude that you know what's going on. Sometimes we can be very confident that we are right about something, only to find later that we were speaking out of our own bluster or momentum.

Remember Samuel at Jesse's house? He was about to anoint the next king of Israel, and God had spoken to him that the future king was one of Jesse's sons. When Samuel saw Eliab, he said to himself, "Sure enough, Eliab's the one!" The Lord said to Samuel, "No, you're wrong. You're looking at the outward appearance of things. The Lord looks at the heart" (1 Sam. 16:6-7 paraphrased). Samuel was God's prophet, and he missed it!

It is said of our Messiah that he "will not judge by what he sees with his eyes, or decide by what he hears with his ears" (Is. 11:3b). He wants us to learn his way.

Before speaking the truth, wait for insight and the right timing. As we listen, God will give insight, maybe a word to share. Then the question becomes: "Is it for now, or later." One time, the Lord gave me an insight into a friend of mine, but I had to sit on it for months before he was ready to hear it. That's a good discipline for all of us. "Judge nothing before the appointed time; wait till the Lord comes" (1 Cor. 4:5).

Speaking the truth means affirming what God is doing. It is as much about recognizing virtue in someone as anything else.

"Nathanael - now there's a man without guile" (John 1:47). Jesus was affirming a characteristic about his new friend and disciple, Nathanael. Catch someone doing good and praise them. That's speaking the truth in love. "I've noticed that you have a special compassion toward those who are deeply wounded. Have you ever considered that you may have a ministry to those people?" A word like that could encourage and re-direct someone's life.

Larry Crabb tells the story of a young woman who stood before a group of residents and parents as part of a recovery weekend. "With trembling lips and tears of shame streaming down her face, she said, 'I've been a prostitute for the last three years. I am so sorry.'

Her father came to the front, embraced the shaking girl and said, 'When I look at you, I see no prostitute in you. You've been washed. I see my beautiful daughter.'"

Can you imagine the power of a group of people who regularly practiced speaking the truth in love? It would truly be a healing community!

Rediscovering the Table Together

How can we become healing communities? Not only by speaking the truth in love, but by sharing common meals together with face-to-face conversations. In the early church, it says, "they devoted themselves to the apostles' teaching and to the fellowship, to the breaking of bread and to prayer" (Acts 2:42), and that "they broke bread in their homes and ate together with glad and sincere hearts" (vs. 46).

Randy Frazee points outs: "There is something vitally important and special about sharing a meal together. Just consider the fact that the Lord's Supper (an act of partaking together of food and drink) is one of the few New Testament rituals we are commanded to observe."[20]

And the manner in which they ate together was *with glad and sincere hearts*. Our table times should include hearty conversation and laughter. Somehow we need to remove the stale institutionalism from communion and see it again as joyful feasting together. Call me a heretic, but I, for one, think this is more likely to happen around a family table than at a church facility's altar.

Mealtime conversation brings a distinctive element of *life* into our relationships. Don't ever think that the only thing we should be talking about with one another is spiritual truths. Along with being spiritual,

---

[20]   *The Connecting Church*, pg. 131 (Zondervan, 2001).

God made us to be intellectual, emotional, physical and social. We should be sharing our lives, our hopes and dreams, the funny ironies we face daily, and our concerns for our families, our communities and our nations.

Our bonding with one another should not just be along some narrow body of shared Biblical truth, but should be as broad as life itself. Remember, Jesus is not only the truth, he is the life (John 14:6)!

Prayer

"Breaking of bread and prayer..." They ate together and they prayed together. This is fascinating to me! I think it's a very natural thing to segue from glad and sincere conversations at the table to praying with one another. Try it. It's really just including God directly in our conversation.

One of the men in our group told me that it took him off guard a bit at how we would be talking to each other and then the next minute begin praying. It's so easy for prayer to become a heavy religious obligation. But really, learning to pray is very similar to learning to converse with one another. Prayer is primarily a relationship, not a duty.

Here's an example of segueing from hearty fellowship into prayer. Years ago, I was part of a celebration feast at the Grange Hall in Santa Ynez, California. Along with enjoying great food, we enjoyed the music of a live county/folk band that was part of the fellowship. And then, some of us got out on the floor and clogged, or, in my case, tried to clog. We ate, we laughed, we danced. At the end, most of us were out of breath.

As we were finishing, the meal and celebration led very naturally to unplanned prayer. When we turned to the Lord just to give him thanks for the evening, someone asked if we could pray that God would send rain. That part of California was in the middle of a serious three year drought. So, in the context of gratitude and celebration, we prayed that God would send rain. And we prayed just as heartily as we had feasted and celebrated.

Guess what? The next day it began raining. It rained and it rained and it rained! Cachuma Lake, the water supply for Santa Barbara which the experts had said would take months to fill back up, filled up in 72 hours!

In *koinonia*, I believe we discover a new facet of prayer: that prayer is conversation with God in the context of relationship.

In our relationships, let's learn to speak the truth in love. Let's rediscover the joy of the table and prayer. Let's become a network of healing communities where miracles happen.

In the next lesson, we are going to learn that *koinonia* is contagious.

Declaration: Together we declare that we will learn to speak powerful healing words to one another. We declare that isolation and loneliness among the people of God will be replaced by hearty fellowship in which the table is celebrated and prayer becomes joyous conversation instead of weary obligation!

Review Question:

Q9.   What three practices will help us become healing communities? What is involved in the first of these practices. (See pages 44-47)

A9.   _____

      _____

      _____

      _____

(Write out your answers then compare with answers at the end of this booklet)

Lesson 8   - Koinonia is Contagious

> Our relationship with each other is the criterion the world uses to judge whether our message is truthful - Christian community is the final apologetic. Francis Shaeffer

It sometimes happens that a tight-knit fellowship can become ingrown and insular.[21] So, in this lesson we want to look at how our experience of *koinonia* relates to our commission to share the good news with others. What I think we'll find is that true fellowship, *koinonia*, is the very thing that makes sharing our faith with others natural and effective. *Koinonia*, as it turns out, is highly contagious!

Let's look at how life together expanded in the early church.

> They broke bread in their homes and ate together with glad and sincere hearts, praising God and enjoying the favor of all the people. And the Lord added to their number daily those who were being saved (Acts 2:46).

The joy, sincerity and togetherness of these early believers created credibility among those in the "watching world." It was, as Shaeffer said, the "final apologetic," the most powerful argument that the gospel is true. *Koinonia* provides a *demonstration* of the kingdom of God, which is much more persuasive than a mere *explanation*.

When people *see* God's kingdom demonstrated through lives lived together, it awakens, in them, a deep aspiration for belonging that all of us have. It excites hope, and opens us up to believe. The writer of Ecclesiastes says that God has "set eternity in the hearts of men" (3:11). Seeing lives lived for God together gives strong evidence to those with seeking hearts that their deepest longings can be fulfilled.

You've probably heard that the biggest obstacle people have in becoming Christians is perceived hypocrisy among those who say they believe. If, on the other hand, there are those who are walking together in the light, forsaking pretense and learning to be real, that fellowship becomes highly believable! The sincerity and genuineness of these

---

[21]   Insular = ignorant of or uninterested in cultures, ideas, or peoples outside one's own experience.

early believers resulted in goodwill from the people around them (Acts 2:46).

God is Light

Look with me at the amazing connection between the essential message of the gospel and the resulting togetherness that the apostle John describes in 1 John 1.

> This is the message we have heard from him and declare to you: God is light; in him there is no darkness at all. If we claim to have fellowship with him yet walk in the darkness, we lie and do not live by the truth. But if we walk in the light, as he is in the light, we have fellowship (*koinonia*) with one another, and the blood of Jesus, his Son, purifies us from all sin.
>
> If we claim to be without sin, we deceive ourselves and the truth is not in us. If we confess our sins, he is faithful and just and will forgive us our sins and purify us from all unrighteousness. If we claim we have not sinned, we make him out to be a liar and his word has no place in our lives.
> 1 John 1:5-7

The message is that God is light, and that he invites us to walk in his light. Walking in the light is not just about correct believing, but about being honest and truthful. The alternative is walking in darkness, or dishonesty, with God and one another.

Honesty and truthfulness with God are inseparably linked with honesty and truthfulness with others. Denying, or covering our sins leads to broken fellowship both with God and with others, and we become isolated. Purification and cleansing cannot result without honesty and truthfulness. Acknowledging our sins by confession to God and others restores us to God's light. It's all there in that first chapter of First John.

Hypocrisy, in the Greek language, means *play-acting*, or *pretending*. When we are involved with close relationships in Christ, those tendencies will be exposed so we can put them behind us. Without close relationships, it's easy to pretend.

Summing up the last three paragraphs, <u>the message - God is light - creates honest relationships with God and with one another</u>. The resulting lack of pretense wins us an audience with those who are yet to believe.

Listen to this example of community evangelism from an interview with Randy Frazee:

> On our street we have two families that have been part of a number of things our home group does together. They are now coming to the church and their kids are involved... So, what we're seeing is not so much "one-on-one" evangelism but community evangelism—where we do more of life together. When believers do more of life together, they don't have to do anything that special; the way of Jesus pervades the way they talk to each other, care for their children, and so on. As unbelievers float in and out of our community life, they are a part of all that, and then many of them come to Christ.
>
> That happened to my neighbor, Roger, who lives diagonally across from me. He came to Christ two years ago. He's about 55 years old, very successful, with grown children. He was fully involved in everything we were doing, and then finally came to terms with deciding to follow Jesus.

A while back, there was a survey that asked those who had become Christians what had been the primary influence that led them to Christ. Among the choices were: 1) evangelistic preaching and 2) the testimony of another person (or persons) in their lives. Nine out of ten said #2, the testimony of others, was the primary influence.

In my coming to Christ, that was definitely the case. It was primarily my roommate in college, Bob Sutton, and his Christian friends, that influenced me to become a Christian.

There's still no better means of evangelism than people telling people. And there's no more receptive audience than those who know that you are *for real*. The gospel radiates out through networks of honest relationships.

Learning about Oikos

There's a Greek word in the New Testament which is translated *house*, *household, family* or *dwelling.* It is *oikos.* For example, Phil. 4:22 - "All the saints send you greetings, especially those who belong to Caesar's household" *(oikos).*

A household, in the Roman world, would consist of the family, and, in some cases, the workers (servants) involved in the business of that family. So *oikos* is a word that can include family members and work relationships.

Oikos has become a sociological term that refers to <u>those with whom you interact on a regular basis - those family members, friends, neighbors and co-workers that make up your sphere of influence or relational context.</u> Here's a picture.

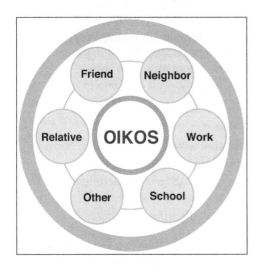

Your *oikos* will include Christians and non-Christians. "Greet those in the household (*oikos*) of Narcissus who are in the Lord" (Rom. 16:11). In the household of Narcissus were those who believed and those who didn't.

Why is this important? <u>Your current sphere of influence, your *oikos*, is where you are going to be most effective in sharing your faith.</u>

You don't have to go half way around the world to evangelize. God does call some to do that. But more likely, God will use you in your existing set of relationships, among those whom you already know. It will be among those you see regularly, and those whom God brings along your path. Imagine the impact if every Christian took seriously the gospel opportunities within his *oikos*!

We all have different callings. There are some who are called as evangelists. They have a knack of meeting strangers and communicating the good news.

But all of us are called to let our lights shine. What you learn in your *koinonia* group, practice it in your *oikos*. Invite those in your *oikos* to do things with your community group. Invite them to share a meal, or go hiking, or whatever, with your fellowship buddies. Let them see what life together in Christ is like. Let them *see* the message, not just *hear* it.

If we let it, *koinonia* will become contagious!

Declaration: We commit ourselves to the practice of walking honestly before God and our brothers and sisters. We also commit ourselves to letting our lights shine before those that God has sovereignly placed in and around our lives.

Review Questions:

Q 10. What is one of the most important characteristics of a group that gives it credibility with those outside the group? How do we acquire that characteristic? (See pages 49-50)

A 10. _____

_____

_____

_____

Q 11.   What is your *oikos*? (See page 52)

A 11.   _____

_____

_____

(Write out your answers then compare with answers at the end of this booklet)

Lesson 9 - What Shall We Do?

> Once upon a time there was a man named Sam who was fed up with the institutional church... So he gathered together a small group of like-minded friends. "We're going to throw out all the institutionalism and have a simple, unstructured New Testament church," said Sam.
>
> They all got together one Sunday evening. Eleven of them. They spent about two-and-a-half hours together just sharing, singing, praying and studying the Bible. Everyone was excited... The group felt drawn together and spiritually strengthened. This was what church was meant to be!
>
> And so a new fellowship was born. The group grew, diversified somewhat and met various needs as they arose. What about child care? What about time and length of meetings? What about leadership? In each case, arrangements were worked out so that the group could function smoothly and would not have to keep making the same minor decisions over and over again.
>
> It worked. The group prospered.
>
> But was it "unstructured," as Sam initially hoped? Of course not. The group quickly developed its own structures... Perhaps the forms adopted were better than those they left behind, serving the true purpose of the church. But structures did indeed appear, for all life must have form.[22]

"All life must have form."

In this 9th and final Lesson in our study of *The Koinonia Ethos*, we need to carefully navigate from understanding an ethos of community to implementing that ethos, which will involve some plan of action, some form, and some organization.

Many of us, including me, are wary of any discussion of organization or structures, because we've seen how structures can often take on a life of their own, leaving behind the original values and beliefs that formed

---

[22] Synder, Howard, *The Community of the King*, chapter 9 (2004, InterVarsity Press, Downers Grove, IL)

them. I've seen this happen in companies as well as churches. Let's always keep alert to that dangerous tendency, but let's not be stymied from action because of a fear of failure.

Just because there are a lot of failed marriages shouldn't make us avoid marriage. Instead we should be all the more diligent to learn how to make marriages work. And just because many who set out to implement an ethos ended up creating structures that completely forgot the ethos, doesn't mean that we have to.

If the purpose of the church is to make disciples who make disciples[23] who affect the world by sharing their faith and letting their lights shine[24] into the cultures of man, and if some structures better accomplish these purposes than others, the simple question should be "which types of organization best serve the mandate of the gospel?"[25]

As you set out to take action, be wary of "anti-institutional" attitudes. In his comparison of movements and institutions,[26] Tim Keller helps us to understand how the two serve different purposes but can help support one another. His wisdom in this served as a corrective for me. Movements are better at certain things; institutions are better at other things. How can we serve one another?

The following thoughts are meant to encourage you to take the first steps of forming a koinonia-type group, or to help you rebuild your existing group into a koinonia-type group.

---

[23]   "Disciple the nations" - Mt. 28:19-20

[24]   "Let you light shine before men…" Mt. 5:14-16.

[25]   For a very thorough discussion of this issue, read the 9th chapter of Howard Snyder's *The Community of the King* (2004, InterVarsity Press, Downers Grove, IL), or his book, *Radical Renewal, The Problem of Wineskins Today* (1996, Touch Publications).

[26]   Keller, Timothy. *Center Church*. Zondervan. 2012. Chapter 27.

Meetings

If you are thinking of starting a *koinonia group* but aren't sure what to do in the meetings or how they should be led, here are some recommendations.

- Look for 3 or 4 others who have an interest in growing together in the Lord. Ask them to pray about meeting together weekly for a limited period of time.

- Decide on a location and a format. It could be as simple as this: Scripture Reading & Listening - Worship - Short Talk - Discussion - Prayer.

- Your group may want to adopt a Bible reading plan like *The Saint James Daily Devotional Guide*. Prepared by Patrick Henry Reardon, this plan takes you through the Bible once every 2 years and references the historic calendar of the church. The quarterly print version is $15 annually. A downloadable copy of the current quarter is available at http://www.fsj.org/ddg-epub/

- Small group meetings are different than larger group meetings. They're not meant to be miniature congregation meetings. They are relationship-building in nature. Make room for conversation and sharing. Everyone in your group has been given gifts. Identify the endeavors God is putting in each others' hearts. Pray for one another.

- Whatever teaching you have, keep it conversational. The style of teaching you'll find in Scripture is much less pedantic than we are used to. You can see this in how Jesus, as a boy, sat among the teachers, "listening to them and asking them questions" (Luke 2:46). It was generally how he taught as well (See Luke 5:30-35, for instance).

- As your meeting develops a committed core, think about others that could be added. But rather than just recruiting others to grow your group, reach out to see how you can bless someone else's life. Most people will welcome that.

Leadership

Don't be afraid of recognizing those among you that have gifts of leadership. Families have leaders; businesses have leaders; armies have leaders; teams have leaders. It's natural and essential to have leaders.

As Randy Frazee pointed out, leadership helps insure common purpose, without which there will be no true community. But, please, don't try to make your leaders into more than they are meant to be.

Leaders are coordinators and facilitators, much like a quarterback or point guard in sports - very important, but not meant to do everything. They are there to equip others to do the work of ministry. They should be team builders. Good leaders stimulate participation, not quench it. One of the most important functions of a biblical leader is to recognize and encourage the gifts among those they lead.

And because no one is above the temptation to misuse power, all of our leaders should be examples of being teachable and submissive. I love the story of Abraham and Melchizedek. Abraham was a great man, one of the most powerful men of his generation. He was known among kings. But when he met Melchizedek, one of the most intriguing characters in Scripture, Abraham instinctively knew that he was in the presence of someone greater than himself. He knew he should give him a tribute, a tenth of all he had, as an offering. Abraham exemplified humble leadership. God give us such leaders!

One other reminder about leadership from the words of Jesus: "The greatest among you will be your servant. For whoever exalts himself will be humbled, and whoever humbles himself will be exalted." (Mt. 23:11,12). Kingdom leadership is very different than worldly leadership.

Listen to this description of Job (before all his troubles): When he took his seat at the city gate, young men stepped aside, old men rose to their feet and the chief men refrained from speaking (29:7-10). Why was he held in such honor?

> Whoever heard me spoke well of me, and those who saw me commended me, because I rescued the poor who cried for help, and the fatherless who had none to assist him. The man who was dying blessed me; I made the widow's heart sing. I put on righteousness as my clothing; justice was my robe and my turban. I was eyes to the blind

> and feet to the lame. I was a father to the needy; I took up
> the case of the stranger. I broke the fangs of the wicked
> and snatched the victims from their teeth. Job 29:11-17.

Eyes to the blind, feet to the lame, a father to the needy. Want to be a
leader? Set aside all your books on leadership and go out to bless,
protect and care for as many as you can. Here's a great test for
leadership: *have you made the widow's heart sing?*

Networking

Cultivate relationship with other similar fellowship groups and group
leaders. Learn from them; encourage them. In time, you may see a
presbytery of group leaders form. Establish a monthly meeting of
group leaders. Pray for each other.

Rent a meeting place or church facility, and bring your groups together
once a month or once a quarter. Share your resources among the
groups. (Remember, *koinonia* means sharing.)

Also, take time to network with other established Christian leaders in
your city or town. Let them know what you're doing. Invite them to
speak into your life as you venture out. Be respectful and teachable
toward them. We are all part of the body of Christ. We need one
another. And as darkness increases in our culture, we will need one
another even more!

What Shall We Do?

The day of Pentecost, in Acts 2, was the Grand Opening of the New
Covenant Community. And it was quite a day! A sound from heaven
was heard all across the city of Jerusalem, a sound like a violent rushing
wind. Visible flames of fire were seen on the heads of those early
disciples in the upper room. They spoke in other languages that they
didn't know, and onlookers from many other countries understood
what they were saying.

But the Holy Spirit wasn't finished with his miracles that day. When
Peter stood up and explained what was going on, the Holy Spirit
convicted the hearts of the listeners and they cried out to Peter and the
other leaders, "Brothers, what shall we do?"

"What shall we do?" The perfect question! Not just "what should we believe?" "What shall we do?"

The answer that day was about how to join this New Community: "Repent and be baptized. Receive forgiveness for your sins in Jesus' name. Receive the Holy Spirit. Disengage from the generation's corruption" (Acts 2:38, 40).

They lined up to be baptized - 3,000 of them! They received forgiveness, they received the Holy Spirit. They left behind an old way of corrupting, self-centered living. As Paul would later write, they were "transferred out of the domain of darkness into the kingdom of God's dear Son" (Col. 1:13).

They were barely dry from the waters of baptism, and little households formed. "They devoted themselves to the apostles' teachings and to the *koinonia*, and to the breaking of bread and prayer" (Acts 2:42). They met in large groups at the temple, and in small groups in their homes. They joyfully shared meals together. They shared their possessions with anyone who had needs. They were "praising God and enjoying the favor of all the people. And the Lord added to their number daily those who were being saved" (Acts 2:47).

A great, history-changing adventure had begun, an adventure that God invites us to join 21 centuries later, an adventure of *life together*.

"What shall we do?"

It's not enough to *learn* about this New Community. There's something to *do*. Walk through the door. Come in out of the dark and into the light. Introduce yourself. Sit down at the table. Meet your new circle of friends. Find out what's going on.

James puts it like this: "Do not merely listen to the word, and so deceive yourselves. Do what it says" (James 1:22).

In this 9th Lesson, we come to a decision time. Are we going to do something in our spheres of life to actively engage in *koinonia*? Or will we just say something like, "I'm so glad I studied *koinonia*: I am much more knowledgeable of the subject than I was before," and then do nothing? I believe better of you.

> Declaration: As Jesus laid his life down for us, we will, by his grace, lay our lives down for others. We will do what we have learned to do!

Review Question:

Q12. What action is God asking me to take to build *koinonia*? (For ideas, see pages 56-59)

A12. _____

_____

_____

(Write out your answers then compare with answers at the end of this booklet)

****

Invitation

Would you do this? As you takes steps into this ethos, share what's happening in your oikos with me. I'd like to share your stories with others. Send them to gg@worshipschools.com.

Also, send me your email if you'd like to receive occasional email updates, and/or if you'd like to learn about hosting or attending a *Koinonia Weekend Retreat*.

Thanks,

Gerrit Gustafson

Review Questions & Answers

Q1.   What is *koinonia*? (See page 5)

A1.   Koinonia is people living their lives together in Christ
      where independence is exchanged for interdependence,
      and sacrificial love for one another is practiced.

> Key Scripture:
>
> They devoted themselves to the apostles' teaching and
> to the fellowship (*koinonia*), to the breaking of bread and
> to prayer. (Acts 2:42)

Q2.   How do I begin to experience *koinonia*? (See page 6 & 7)

A2.   Identify that circle of friends that God has intended for
      you. Begin with two or three, and ask God to help you
      love them like he loves you.

> Key Scriptures:
>
> This is how we know what love is: Jesus Christ laid
> down his life for us. And we ought to lay down our lives
> for our brothers (1 John 3:16).
>
> Do nothing out of selfish ambition or vain conceit, but
> in humility consider others better than yourselves. Each
> of you should look not only to your own interests, but
> also to the interests of others. (Phil. 2:3-4)

Q3.   What does it mean to be a disciple of Jesus? (See pages
      9-12)

A3.   A disciple of Jesus is someone who has made a deep-
      level commitment to choose God's will over any other
      thing, person or ambition. A disciple of Jesus is
      someone who is learning 1) to live by the Word of God,

2) to walk in the Holy Spirit and 3) to be accountable to others.

Key Scriptures:

Anyone who comes to me but refuses to let go of father, mother, spouse, children, brothers, sisters - yes, even one's own self! - can't be my disciple. Anyone who won't shoulder his own cross and follow behind me can't be my disciple.

Simply put, if you're not willing to take what is dearest to you, whether plans or people, and kiss it good-bye, you can't be my disciple. (Luke 14:26-27, 33, *The Message*)

Man does not live on bread alone, but on every word that comes from the mouth of God. (Mt. 4:4)

Live by the Spirit, and you will not gratify the desires of the sinful nature. (Gal. 5:16)

Confess your sins to each other and pray for each other so that you may be healed. (James 5:16)

Q4.   How can we begin to know what God's plan for our lives is? (See pages 16-19)

A4.   We will know God's will for us when we 1) unconditionally surrender to do whatever he wants, 2) learn faithfulness in what he gives us to do, and 3) begin to give away to others what he has given us.

Key Scriptures:

If anyone chooses to do God's will, he will find out whether my teaching comes from God or whether I speak on my own. (John 7:17)

Whoever can be trusted with very little can also be trusted with much, and whoever is dishonest with very little will also be dishonest with much. So if you have not been trustworthy in handling worldly wealth, who will trust you with true riches? And if you have not been trustworthy with someone else's property, who will give you property of your own? (Luke 16:10-12)

Give, and it will be given to you. A good measure, pressed down, shaken together and running over, will be poured into your lap. For with the measure you use, it will be measured to you (Luke 6:38).

Q5.   What is the doctrine of the Headship of Christ? (See page 21)

A5.   It is the truth that Jesus Christ leads the church much like the head of a body directs the whole body, that the government of the church is on his shoulders, not ours, and that he will actively lead his church if we let him.

Key Scriptures:

For to us a child is born, to us a son is given, and the government will be on his shoulders… Of the increase of his government and peace there will be no end. (Is. 9:6-7)

We will in all things grow up into him who is the Head, that is, Christ. (Ep. 4:15)

Q6.   What is the secret of church growth found in Ephesians 4:15-16? (See pages 22-23)

A6.   The church grows spontaneously 1) as we speak the truth to one another in love, and 2) as each member actively does his part.

Key Scripture:

Instead, speaking the truth in love, we will in all things grow up into him who is the Head, that is, Christ. From him the whole body, joined and held together by every supporting ligament, grows and builds itself up in love, as each part does its work. (Eph. 4:15-16)

Q7. Why were the gifts of the Spirit given to the church? (See page 30)

A7. God gave us spiritual gifts to equip us to serve other and make known the manifold grace of God.

Key Scripture:

Each one should use whatever gift (*charisma*) he has received to serve others, faithfully administering God's grace (*charis*) in its various forms. (I Pet. 4:10)

Q8. What are the three elements that make small groups into communities? Explain each. (See pages 36-37)

A8. Common purpose, common place and common possessions. *Common purpose* happens when our individual plans and purposes are subjected to an agreed-upon central purpose. *Common place* happens when we live our lives in close proximity with one another and see each other frequently. *Common possessions* happens when we begin to share our resources with others.

Key Scripture:

Selling their possessions and goods, they gave to anyone as he had need. Every day they continued to meet together in the temple courts. They broke bread in their

homes and ate together with glad and sincere hearts.
Acts 2:46

Q9.   What three practices will help us become healing
      communities? What is involved in the first of these
      practices. (See pages 44-47)

A9.   Truth speaking, sharing meals together and prayer.
      Truth speaking requires respecting, listening, waiting
      and affirming.

Key Scriptures:

Therefore encourage one another and build each other
up. 1 Thess. 5:11

When he was at the table with them, he took bread,
gave thanks, broke it and began to give it to them.
Then their eyes were opened and they recognized him.
Luke 24:31

Q10. What is one of the most important characteristics of a
      group that gives it credibility with those outside the
      group? How do we acquire that characteristic? (See
      page 49)

A10. Genuineness in our relationships. We acquire that
      characteristic when we walk in the light together, which
      simply means walking in honesty before God and one
      another.

Key Scripture:

They broke bread in their homes and ate together with
glad and sincere hearts, praising God and enjoying the
favor of all the people. And the Lord added to their
number daily those who were being saved. Acts 2:46-47

If we claim to have fellowship with him yet walk in the
darkness, we lie and do not live by the truth. 1 John 1:6

Q11.   What is your *oikos*? (See page 52)

A11.   My *oikos* is my sphere of relationships with whom I
interact on a regular basis. It includes family members,
friends, neighbors and co-workers . These are the ones
with whom I will most likely be able to communicate
my faith effectively.

Q12.   What action is God asking me to take in order to build
koinonia? Be specific. (see Pages 56-59)

A12.   There will be many different answers to this question,
but as you listen for the Lord's instruction, ask him
about leadership and about forming or joining a group.
Is he calling you to take leadership with others? Is there
someone he has brought into your life to help lead you?
Is he directing you to begin a meeting? Or if you are
already meeting, would he have you network with other
koinonia groups?

Key Scripture:

Then I heard the voice of the Lord saying, "Whom
shall I send? And who will go for us?" And I said, "Here
am I. Send me!" Isaiah 6:8

"Come follow me," Jesus said. Matthew 4:19

About the Author

*Since his conversion in college, Gerrit Gustafson has worn many hats - church
planting pastor/teacher, church music director, songwriter, producer, publisher, writer
and businessman. He and his wife, Himmie, have five children and live in the
Nashville area.*

56012947R00040

Made in the USA
Middletown, DE
20 July 2019